RICH WIF1 HUSBAND

BY

Pastor Nandir Williams

Published By

Kratos Publisher

Dedication

I would like to dedicate this book to three women who have been mentors in my marriage journey. My mother, Chief Mrs Anne Banfa, Pastor Charity Dina and Rev Teju Alonge. Thank ou may God continue to use you to bless others.

Content

Introduction

In this book, we will be dealing with the challenges and struggles we face in marriage. I want to start by acknowledging my husband, who usually works tirelessly in the background whilst we are in the studio. He is my sweetheart and the only sugar in my tea. He is continually coordinating and has been a massive part of the treasures for living team from the beginning. So even though I am journaling my experience, this is a shared journey with my husband.

Here is a story I would love to start with;

An African man owed his children school fees, and they were due for payment. However, he did not have money or any financial capacity to pay the school fees, even when the school had been asking and pressuring him to pay. Unknown to him his wife had paid the school fees and instructed the school not to reveal this payment to her husband. I believe that from the story, the man had finished work on the day the school fees were due, and since he struggled to pay, he ended up jumping off the bridge and committing suicide.

Whilst I was discussing this story with a friend, we could express the sad feelings this story invoked in us. So we concluded that the lack of communication between this couple sadly led to the death and loss of a family member. Can you imagine this situation? What will happen when the children find out how their dad died? How would this make them feel? What kind of example is this incident to society? How would the wife feel? Should money, no matter how much it is worth, lead to the death of your spouse? I mentioned this story not to judge anybody, as non of us are in their shoes. Nowadays, I try to empathise with individuals letting them know I understand and appreciate where they are coming from. I don't know precisely the full details of the incident from their perspective. Although this made me realise the benefit of talking about the struggles, difficulties and challenges we have in our marriages.

Marriage is a gift from God, it is a union of two people whom God intends to be one. I recently watched a race where a blind athlete was running and she was tied to another person who was helping her fun. As they both ran in sync and with prupose and determination they won the race. That is what we are called to do in marriage, help each other succeed it looked so inspiring as they both ran and she matched his speed. The pair of them won the race, it was a beautiful picture to behold. It spoke of two people in a loving and supportive friendship God called us to support one another in the union of marriage. God does not call us to compete but to complement one another. As you read this little book may God help you to complement and not compete in your relationships.

In The Beginning

God is the author of marriage, the one who authored homes and relationships, and we can see that God didn't create man to work for him. He created man for relationships. The Bible says in the Book of Genesis that in the evening, in the cool of the evening, God will come into the garden to fellowship with Adam and Eve. Your Father created you for fellowship, So the same way God created us for fellowship is the same way God wants us to interact with others.

In fellowship, so Genesis, God authored marriage genesis Genesis 1:26

(Gen 1:26) And God said, Let us make man in our image, after our likeness: and let them have dominion over the fish of the sea, and over the fowl of the air, and over the cattle, and over all the earth, and over every creeping thing that creepeth upon the earth

Then God said, let us, Father, Son and Holy Spirit, make man in our image. You are made in the image of God! According to our likeness, not physical but a spiritual personality. So you are not physical, no matter what the devil tells you, you're not physical; you are a spiritual personality and moral likeness. So God created us, so we will be like him spiritually, we will be like him morally notice, He doesn't talk about us being like him physically And let them. So He creates man, and then he says "THEM".

I once interviewed Bishop Bob Alonge, and on our series, he spoke about the realm of them.

It says, and let them have complete authority, so he says, to man and woman Not just to man, It says let them have complete authority, Over the fish of the sea, the birds of the air, the cattle and over the entire earth and over everything that creeps and crawls on the earth. So God created man in his own image, No matter what the devil tells you about how you look, your nose, or your legs.

So God created man in His own image. In the image and likeness of God, He created him, Male and female, He created them. God created male, and he created female; this was God's idea. Verse 28, and God blessed them! Notice He didn't say God blessed the woman, and He didn't say He blessed the man. He says God blessed THEM. When it came to marriage, yesterday we interviewed Reverend Matthew and one of the things he said, he said when we are in a marriage, we need to be thinking about us, not I, us, not I, We, not I; it says God bless them, granting them certain authority God bless them, Adam and Eve, granting them certain authority and said to them; be fruitful, multiply and fill the earth and subjugate it.

God said to them to both man and woman, it is a commandment, it is a command, God wants us to be fruitful, and that's why anytime you're not fruitful, anytime you're not progressing. Anytime you're not increasing, There's discomfort within your Spirit because God designed and created everybody, even a two-year-old, to be fruitful. It says to be fruitful, multiply and fill the earth and subjugate it, putting it under your power. Now when God starts to talk about putting something under your power, he does not say to put your husband under your power. He does not say to put your wife under your power. He says, be fruitful, multiply and fill the earth. So God is now telling them what to do regarding the earth and subjugate it. Now when it comes to subjugation or exercising dominion over, He does not talk about the realm of THEM. He talks about IT. IT is an object, and subjugate it, putting it under your power and rule over, dominate the fish of the sea. So, Myles Munroe says that the fish of the sea, the birds of the air, and every living thing that moves upon the earth is what God created for dominion. God did not create a race. He did not create a person or a gender to be dominated over. So whether I see a woman dominating the husband or a man dominating a woman, dominion is not exercised when it comes to persons. Dominion is exercised when it comes to, you know, the creatures, creation when it comes to the forces; in the earth, when it comes to the Earth itself, that's when we exercise dominion. The Scripture says that God bless them, granting them certain authority. You know when the devil says you don't have authority, you don't have power, you cannot do, Remember that God has given it to you already; and said to them, be fruitful if you're reading this today, God's word concerning your life is that you'll be fruitful, I speak fruitfulness into your life, that you will multiply. I speak a speaking multiplication into your life, and that you will fill the earth with your giftings, your talent, and you'll subjugate it, Just putting it under your power and rule over, dominate the fish of the sea, the birds of the air, and every living thing that moves upon the earth.

(Gen 1:27) So God created man in his own image, in the image of God created he him; male and female created he them.

(Gen 1:28) And God blessed them, and God said unto them, Be fruitful, and multiply, and replenish the earth, and subdue it: and have dominion over the fish of the sea, and over the fowl of the air, and over every living thing that moveth upon the earth.

(Gen 1:29) And God said, Behold, I have given you every herb bearing seed, which is upon the face of all the earth, and every tree, in the which is the fruit of a tree yielding

seed; to you, it shall be for meat.

(Gen 1:30) And to every beast of the earth, and to every fowl of the air, and to everything that creepeth upon the earth, wherein there is life, I have given every green herb for meat: and it was so.

(Gen 1:31) And God saw everything that he had made, and, behold, it was very good. And the evening and the morning were the sixth day.

So when God created man and woman, He saw that it was good. He validated his creation completely. So we're talking about the origins of marriage, Genesis, where we've read from verse 26 to the end of chapter one that God validated the realm of them, that God saw that the realm of them was good. The Bible says that two are better than one if we really trust and believe God's word that; God knows what He's doing. We trust that God is omniscient, omnipotent, and all-knowing if we trust that God has our best interest at heart, as married couples or even as a single person if you're reading this today. It would be best if you believed in the realm of them. With all that's happening in this day and age now, there is such an attack on homes, there's such an attack on families, and the thing that the Holy Spirit has been saying to me repeatedly, he said, Now as the years' progress and as the days go by, the home is going to come under intense assault. As it comes under intense assault, those of you who are within the walls of the family and home, you need to be ready for the assaults that will come. You know the Bible says that when we hear God's word in Matthew Chapter 7, listening to God's word, We obey that word when we put it into practice. The Bible says that would be like that man that founded his house, built his house upon a rock. The man that built his house on sand and the man that built his house on the rock both built their houses. One built his house on a solid foundation, and The other built it on a foundation that was not solid; they faced the same attack. We need to believe that two are better than one. So, For us to build our homes and our families on a rock-solid foundation, we need to understand and practice God's word. my question to you today is when the storms come, when the winds blow and when the rains fall, are you going to be walking in God's word, believing in the realm of them? Or are you going to be walking contrary? May God help us as we practise God's principles regarding marriage. Remember, there is no substitute for the word of God.

Thinking Right

Thinking right is crucial in marriages, as the enemy uses our thoughts to attack and affect us. I will give you an example then we will explore the scriptures together.

Many years ago, I did something awful and wrong, and for three years, satan reminded me of what I did; he would speak to me about it daily and rehearsed the scenario in my mind; this continued for a long time. But Thank God for obedience, just obeying Scripture. You know, in Joshua chapter one, God tells Joshua that one of the keys to success, Joshua, if you're going to be successful, if you're going to be great, If you're going to fill the shoes of Moses and live long, if you're going not to allow these children of Israel not to kill you before your time, I'm just being naughty, But you know what I mean. He told Joshua, I said, thou shall meditate, that he was to meditate in his word in, in the word day and night, and was to observe, to do all that was written therein. Then it says that when Joshua had done this, Joshua would make his way prosperous and then Joshua would have good success. There's good and bad success, so I decided just to start reading the Bible because God's word says so. I began reading the book of Hebrews, was going through the book of Hebrews, and one day I came across the Scripture that talked about the efficacy of the blood of Jesus and how the blood of Jesus, the sacrifice of Jesus' life, was potent enough, So there's a scripture that talks about if the blood of bulls and goats was sufficient, you know, to wash the sins of the Israelites in the Old Testament, how much more the blood of Jesus, how much more will it speak for me?

(Heb 9:13) For if the blood of bulls and of goats, and the ashes of an heifer sprinkling

the unclean, sanctifieth to the purifying of the flesh:

(Heb 9:14) How much more shall the blood of Christ, who through the eternal Spirit offered himself without spot to God, purge your conscience from dead works to serve the living God?

When I came across the Scripture, I stayed on the verse, I read it, and it was like a bomb went off in my Spirit, Not a bad bomb, It was good. Then as the revelation dawned on me, I stayed in that spot, and I cried and cried, and I cried. After that, the enemy, in his cunning ways, came to me to wind me up. He began the accusations of what I did wrong; how can you call yourself a Christian? This time I had my sword of the Spirit, I had my shield of faith, I pulled out that Scripture, and I wish you were there to see me. I was just quoting it, and then I'll speak; I was binding, casting, and rebuking. So all this while, Well, for three years, I had moments of deep sadness, moments of regret, moments of looking back; I'd lost my confidence about certain things, even my ability to come into the presence of God. Sometimes, when I want to ask God for something, and the devil flashes me with previous thoughts like a flash card, I become humble, and I reduce my prayer point. So I said all of that to say this, and I'm going to read the verses scripture Bible says in proverbs Chapter 23 says, as a man thinks in his heart, so he is. If my thinking is not right, My actions cannot be right. Every action of yours is produced from the thinking, and that's why the devil overkills in this area. Whilst speaking with some of my friends one day, we were laughing, and we said that the devil has his own flicks, his own channel, and his own things that he likes to run. Now my husband, many times when he's teaching us to judge, especially when I was so into my warfare thing, I sadly did not believe my husband. There's something that I've learned from my husband, and he works on his thoughts. He doesn't just let things just run rampage in his mind; at least, that's what I believe from what he says to me. He works on his thoughts; he says he doesn't allow negative thoughts in his mind, and I'm learning. My husband taught us a while ago that warfare Is not just about who does this or that in the atmosphere; he said Spiritual world warfare is about your thinking, how you're thinking, the suggestions of the enemy, his lies, his repetitive lies in your mind, the things that the enemy is saying. So, to buttress that point, let's see an example in Scripture, Whatever problem, you have the answers in the word. We're talking about the realm of them, and we're talking about marriage, how we can work together as couples, how a husband and a wife can experience the blessings, the benefits, and the awesome treasure of walking in the realm of them. How a couple can walk together and realise God's destiny for their lives; when we're no longer individual or individualistic but will become a team, we said God sees us as one! The enemy is against your marriage.

(2Co 10:3) For though we walk in the flesh, we do not war after the flesh:

(2Co 10:4) (For the weapons of our warfare are not carnal, but mighty through God to the pulling down of strong holds;)

(2Co 10:5) Casting down imaginations, and every high thing that exalteth itself against the knowledge of God, and bringing into captivity every thought to the obedience of Christ;

(2Co 10:6) And having in a readiness to revenge all disobedience, when your obedience is fulfilled.

It says for though we walk in the flesh, so we're walking in the flesh, we're walking in the flesh as mortal men. We are not carrying on our spiritual warfare according to the flesh, So anytime you get to engage in fleshly wars, You are not operating in the Spirit. You're not operating in the realm where you should be and using the weapons of man; verse four says the weapons of our warfare are not physical weapons of flesh and blood. So you know, all those techniques people want to use in a marriage are extra-biblical, extrajudicial manipulation, intimidation, control, and all those things. It says the weapons of our warfare are not physical weapons of flesh and blood. Our weapons are divinely powerful, God tells us, says weapons I've given you their powerful they will deliver effect. It says for the destruction of what? Not talking about the witch from your village? Am I saying there are no Witches? There are, But that's not what we are focusing on. It says our weapons are divinely powerful for the destruction of fortresses. So that negative thought you have about marriage, that negative thought you have about your spouse? Oh, they will run away, Ohh, they'll cheat me, Oh they'll make me feel sad, they will hit me. It is the devil! There are times I'm in my house, and I'm just by myself, and the devil will bring me song sheets, Song sheets Oh, you know, your husband did this, He did this, He did this, this, this, this, this, this, this and this And you know, and then the devil tell will me about his motive and the reason why you see he did that, is because he did this. In the past, when I began to yield to those accusations, I began to get weaker, weaker, and weaker, leading me to get angry, angry, angry. So, this is a fortress in your mind. Why don't you investigate that thought about your spouse? Investigate the thought! A while back, I was thinking about a particular situation, and all sorts of thoughts kept coming to my mind; Satan kept telling me the reasons for things happening about a certain individual; they were all bad thoughts.

Anyway, so I decided to investigate. Scriptures say love in First Corinthians 13 believes all things. If we are walking in the realm of them, we need to believe the best concerning our spouse. You know Satan hates your marriage because your marriage to your spouse symbolises Christ and His church. Every time Satan looks at your marriage, he gets angry because of this symbolism of what God has done with His church and what he's doing with his church. Your marriage speaks volumes to heaven and hell. So our weapons are divinely powerful for the destruction of fortresses, We are destroying sophisticated arguments. You know, there are some sophisticated arguments just satan brings my way; he tells me this happened in your in-law's lives so many years ago that it's going to happen to you. Then the Holy Spirit told me, why don't you tell the devil? That look at this, this, this, this, this, this that is not going to happen to you. This happened in your mum's life, and this happened in your dad's life, this happens in XY Z is going to happen to you, Sophisticated arguments! You know, I thank God for the Holy Spirit, The Holy Spirit just brought up examples. He just brought up examples in my Spirit. He said, counteract the lies of the enemy, call his bluff. It says we are destroying sophisticated arguments and every exalted and proud thing that sets itself up against the true knowledge of God. What's the true knowledge of God? His word, His person? His character? His abilities? and we are taking every thought and purpose captive to the obedience of Christ. When the devil or whatever Spirit comes to bring all manner of accusations against your spouse, Tell the devil first one Corinthians 13; love believes all things, Love is kind, Love is patient, Love is long-suffering, does not envy, It does not boast, It is not rude, it is not proud. The devil, he's the one doing overtime. So there are contrary thoughts, thoughts from how you grew up, and movies you watched, like Coronation Street. I am not saying we don't watch Coronation Street, but the movies we watch can form a stronghold in our minds. We are destroying sophisticated arguments and every exalted and prompting thing that sets itself up against the true knowledge of God. We are taking every thought and purpose, so there are thoughts that the enemy will bring and their purposes of the enemy that we have to hold captive, it says Bring them to the obedience of Christ. We're talking about the realm of them. Part of the reason we are having challenges and we're not coming together is that our thinking is wrong. When you're thinking is wrong about the realm of them, About us, About Marriage, You cannot walk in good success, Your marriage will not be successful, But I want to believe, and I want to trust God, that this will not be our portion in Jesus name. We need to investigate our thinking. If your marriage is unimportant, why is satan spending so much time on it? So I want to leave you with this challenge: Investigate your thoughts about your spouse, your thoughts about your union, your thoughts about your team, and your thoughts about your togetherness, investigated! Are you thinking the right thoughts?

Spiritual Warfare and The Flesh

(2Co 10:3) For though we walk in the flesh, we do not war after the flesh:

(2Co 10:4) (For the weapons of our warfare are not carnal, but mighty through God to the pulling down of strong holds;)

(2Co 10:5) Casting down imaginations, and every high thing that exalteth itself against the knowledge of God, and bringing into captivity every thought to the obedience of Christ;

So you're walking in the flesh, as mortal men, we are not carrying on our spiritual warfare according to the flesh. So as we live together, as spouses, husband and wife, we come against challenges, and we come against difficulties when we struggle, quarrel, fight, or argue. When we have difficulties, There's a way? God wants us to resolve our difficulties; He doesn't want us to resolve them as fleshly men, As for though we walk in the flesh as mortal men, we're not carrying on our spiritual warfare according to the flesh and using the weapons of man such as; hatred, intimidation, malice, control, bitterness Anger, slander, those are the weapons of the flesh. I remember one day, I went to talk to our Pastor; a While ago, I discussed this challenge I had with my husband. He told me something very profound; most times, he said profound things to me, never facing me directly, and said to me; You know the devil has authority over the flesh. Then he walked away; I guess he probably was frustrated with my fighting and quarrelling, so he said, the devil has authority over the flesh, and you know what? At that point, I felt called to be an intercessor for a territory, and I used to Pray Pray, Pray for this territory, Pray for revival, Pray for your particular group of people, pray for the ministers in those in those territories. Then

I realised that I was under attack. One day, the Pastor said to me, he said the devil has authority over the flesh, you know, when you operate with the Weapons of the flesh, Satan has dominion in that area. You can never win if you operate in the flesh; you are living your life in the flesh; you're using fleshly techniques to be married to your spouse. Satan has all the dominion; he has absolute dominion when you operate in the flesh. So then I would experience all sorts of attacks, attacks in my dreams, I used to have nightmares, things just happened to me, that doesn't mean that if your life is right, you won't experience attacks, because look, apostle Paul was at sea, was adrift at sea, was beaten with rods a Viper tried to bite him when in a city, they will chase him out, they will stone him, they'll think they've left him for dead. But you know, that's the amazing thing about the Holy Spirit. I don't know why we tend to trust the weapons of the flesh, and forget that when you walk with God, You are unstoppable. Paul is my greatest. Like he's my hero in the New Testament because he overcame great difficulties. Let me tell you about one of the attacks; so I said vastly For though we walk in the flesh as mortal men? We're not carrying on as spiritual warfare according to the flesh using the weapons of man. Yeah, so I'll give an example. Again, Then my husband used to speak to me about certain things, about working together. However, I was so stubborn and rebellious, I was rebellious, I remember looking at this picture where, my husband sitting in the church facing the pulpit. I was sitting in my seat facing the other side, can you Imagine? In church? I was rebellious; no wonder I had all those attacks, no wonder I was suffering, no wonder I was not being blessed; so I'm talking about a rich wife, poor husband. Are you sharing yourself with your spouse? Are you? Are you? What are you bringing to your marriage? Are you bringing your wealth, your joy, your comfort, your love, your giftings, your talents, your anointing? Your help?Are you pouring all of yourself? Are you holding it back? Are you resistant? Are you fighting? Are you rebellious?God says, for though we walk in the flesh as mortal men, We are not carrying on our spiritual warfare according to the flesh and using the weapons of man. So I was using a weapon of man and found all sorts of ways to justify myself, and I was in church; I was even a pastor; how shameful! Let me tell you what happened to me. I had a headache that would not go away, I was praying for the nations, praying for the ministers, praying for revival, but I was rebellious. I'm not listening. I will not submit to my husband and not listen to him. So I had this headache for like three months, and when I say I had a headache, I am talking about the kind that you take medication like paracetamol and yet it remains. So one day, God knows how to capture everybody. One day in my time of devotion, God said to me, " Do you know why you have that headache?I said, No! Then He said it is because you've been rebellious and stubborn to your husband, then He said you need to go and kneel down, You need to go and repent, You should ask him to pray for you, and you need to change. it Sounds like OK. I don't think I went the first day, That's why I think I went the second, because I had all this pride in me and thought if and when I kneeled down when I confessed to him, it would solidify his position, the more. These are all the things that Satan brings to our minds. Yeah, you know, Charles Stanley says we need to obey God and leave the consequences to him. Anyway, So I went to my husband. I knelt down, and I said to him, I'm sorry I've been disobedient, I've been stubborn, and I've been rebellious, I then asked him to forgive me and to pray for me. I told him about the headache, Then he laid his hands on my head and prayed for me. I kid you not! As soon as he took his hands off, the headache was gone! What I struggled with for three months, taking paracetamol and trying to rest, trying to sleep, I did everything, but I still had that headache. Rich wife, poor husband? What are you bringing into the realm of them. The weapons of your warfare, are they fleshly at the carnal? What is spiritual? Remember, satan has authority when it comes to the realm of the flesh. Let the weapons of your warfare in your marriage, Let them be spiritual weapons, weapons of love, joy, peace, patience I, and I'm not saying you don't confront even, when it is there or don't speak up, That's not what

Scripture says There's a balance to everything. We need to ensure that for you, where you stand and as you walk and as you operate in your marriage, you're working in the realm of them. You're doing what God expects. You are bringing your best and working as a team with your spouse.

Not withholding Good

(Pro 3:27) Withhold not good from them to whom it is due, when it is in the power of thine hand to do it.

(Pro 3:28) Say not unto thy neighbour, Go, and come again, and to morrow, I will give; when thou hast it by thee.

(Pro 3:29) Devise not evil against thy neighbour, seeing he dwelleth securely by thee.

So, God says to you and me not to withhold good and keep anything back that is good. God told me to do something for my son, and I kept thinking about several factors, including time. Finally, I asked myself, is this good? Will it bring him closer to Christ? Will it shine the light of Christ in this situation? Once I got yes to all three questions, then I executed what God told me, and I remember him telling me that

Nandir, you have to make sure the light of God shines through your life so that your children will have an example to follow. *(Act 10:38) How God anointed Jesus of Nazareth with the Holy Ghost and with power: who went about doing good, and healing all that were oppressed of the devil; for God was with him.*

The proof of the anointing was the Holy Ghost and power, the result of the anointing and power was Good. So, are you withholding anything in your marriage, home, team, this realm of them, this unit? Are you holding back good things? The Bible says do not withhold good from them to whom it is due. In other words, it's rightful recipient. Is your spouse, husband or wife not the rightful recipient of good? Are you sharing your finances? Are you sharing love? Are you showing mercy? Are you sharing your giftings and talents? Are you supportive and strengthening their hands? Or are you withholding? As the above scripture mentions, there are things in our power to do. We are talking in the context of the realm of them, where we operate and show Christ to the world, coming together as man and woman and doing the things God has called us to do.

So what does God expect from you and me? He expects us not to withhold good when it's in our power to do it, especially to our respective or prospective spouses. For example, when God says to use the finances you have been saving to give to your husband to buy something he wants. And you tell God, Pardon? Or when God says to the husband, you need to buy your wife that dress as you know she desires it even though you have been keeping the funds to purchase a football jersey.

God says;

(Pro 3:28) Say not unto thy neighbour, Go, and come again, and to morrow I will give; when thou hast it by thee.

Do you know why God says not to wait till tomorrow? It is because tomorrow might not be there, I am saying this genuinely and not to manipulate you, but I know from experience.

(Pro 3:29) Devise not evil against thy neighbour, seeing he dwelleth securely by thee.

When getting recycle bins one day, with the biggest smile on my face and deepest politeness I could spring up, I asked my neighbours for more recycle bags. Whilst walking back from that pleasant encounter, I said to myself, Nandir, you are a hypocrite. Is this how you treat your husband? Is this how you treat your children? Are you always this nice? Do you always have this smile? Is this how you treat them? I felt like I got caught! And said to me OK, I need to work on my attitude. It seems easier to be patient with strangers, whilst when my daughter is trying to teach more some new exercises, I get on edge and try to hurry her up, which in turn drives her away, even though I didn't mean to be that way, I just need to be patient.

Here is another example; when we were in Nigeria, a person had given me something precious; well, it happened the next day I realised my husband needed the very thing that was given to me. As you can imagine, when I got caught by God in my prayer time, my most spiritual moment with my hands firmly held together and piety to the most high. God said; you know that thing the person gave you. You need to give it to your husband because he needs it now. I had hidden it in the deepest part of my luggage. I had to bring it out and give it to him. After I pretended not to hear God for a while. After I obeyed, I felt a tremendous release and peace. When God looks at marriages from heaven, He doesn't see two separate beings. He sees one, especially according to Ephesians 5, He calls us one flesh. According to Genesis 2:24

(Gen 2:24) Therefore shall a man leave his Father and his mother, and shall cleave unto his wife: and they shall be one flesh.

You might say to yourself that we are most certainly not one flesh; well I can tell you it takes a while, but when we are committed and dedicated to becoming one flesh, it works. I realise we might have come from homes where we haven't seen one flesh in operation, which might be the root of the strongholds in our minds and issues that affect our perspectives, the struggles we face and the battles we fight.

It might be that when we begin to aim for oneness, that will be the exact time satan will try to remind us of the past failures of our spouse in their relationship with us. This demonstrates the battle against one flesh.

Do good; as you do, goodness will flow from you and surround you. The anointing is found in goodness. I admire a friend of mine called Pastor bimbo, who is a larger-than-life personality and every time she walks in the room, I sometimes feel goosebumps all over my body. She was such a mother who flowed with goodness in everyway and a tremendous example of not withholding good.

(Gal 6:7) Be not deceived; God is not mocked: for whatsoever a man soweth, that shall he also reap.

(Gal 6:8) For he that soweth to his flesh shall of the flesh reap corruption; but he that soweth to the Spirit shall of the Spirit reap life everlasting.

(Gal 6:9) And let us not be weary in well

doing: for in due season we shall reap, if we faint not.

The amplified

7 Do not be deceived, God is not mocked [He will not allow Himself to be ridiculed, nor treated with contempt nor allow His precepts to be scornfully set aside]; for whatever a man sows, this and this only is what he will reap.

(did not include the story about the spouse that left because you were cautious or concerned)

What are we sowing in marriage? What are we sowing regarding affection, compassion, empathy, etc.? God gave me a picture or an example. I had to go all the way to central London to see a demonstration of what God was trying to teach me regarding my own marriage. When God told me he wanted me to do what I saw, I was resistant, and in that very moment, I saw the pride in my heart and how it had affected my spouse, myself and my children.

God is serious when He mentions in the scriptures that God blessed them and said to them, Also, when the Scripture says He made the two to become one flesh. What are you sowing into your marriage? Because the Bible says do not be deceived. The day to reap is coming. There are some challenges that I have reaped, and when I realised I had a quick heart adjustment, repentance, by the way, is not when you are crying, but when there is a change and turn around where you say God help me, I am going to be committed to making a change, irrespective of the cost. God does not care if you think other people have pride, whether they are your spouse, boss or children. God cares about making you Holy. So God says to me, YOU, Nandir, YOU! You be a good wife.

Rich Wife Poor Husband

If you withhold good from your spouse, it's exactly what leads to Rich Wife, Poor Husband or Rich Husband, Poor Wife.

Conclusion

Marriage was not created for you, the husband or the wife; marriage was created for God and meant to reflect Christ's relationship between Him and The Church. So when we operate in a marriage, we have to share all that is ours, Like Jesus shares all He has with the church. When we Look at the book of Ephesians chapters 1-3, we get excited about the precious truths revealed therein, such as; we receive redemption through the blood of Christ, we are accepted in the beloved, he made known to us the counsel of his will, we have been predestinated, new creation realities. This is because when we come to God, we now become a part of His body. Do you remember those covenant words you took when you got married? What you did is that you will share your life; the Bible talks about our fellowship, our communion, and our walk with God. The Bible says that in

Him (God), we live, move, and have our being. Colossians says we are complete in Him, who is the head of all principalities and all powers. Everything that tries to tell you that you are not enough is lying! You are enough when you come and give your life to God. You are not enough because of yourself, your gift or your talents. You are enough because God says you are enough. It seems we want to be like Jesus and the church when it comes to power and revelation, but we don't want to be like Jesus and the Church when it comes to sharing. We can see from Scripture that God created man and shared His life with man, He released His breath into man, and man became a living being! Acts chapter talks about the Holy Spirit and how they tarried to receive the Spirit because when you spend time with the Holy Spirit, you get baptised with the Holy Spirit. That is God's strength and ability within you, So God shares everything with you, including His own Spirit. Ephesians 1:3 says we have been blessed with all spiritual blessings in the heavenly realms. Not that we will be blessed; we are already blessed because Jesus died on the cross.

3

'Why have we fasted,' they say, 'and You do not see it? Why have we humbled ourselves and You do not notice? Hear this [O Israel], on the day of your fast [when you should be grieving for your sins] you find something you desire [to do], And you force your hired servants to work [instead of stopping all work, as the law teaches].

So these people fasted, and God didn't see it; they cried for help, and God didn't see it. They were basically doing their own thing. They were disobedient to God.

4

"The facts are that you fast only for strife and brawling and to strike with the fist of wickedness.

You do not fast as you do today to make your voice heard on high.

These people were fasting, quarrelling and striking, so there is a way we can fast that our voices will be heard on high, and there is a way we fast, and our voices will not be heard on high. I don't know about you, but I want my voice to be heard on high.

5

"Is a fast such as this what I have chosen, a day for a man to humble himself [with sorrow in his soul]? Is it only to bow down his head like a reed And to make sackcloth and ashes as a bed [pretending to have a repentant heart]?

Do you call this a fast and a day pleasing to the LORD?

These people are doing all the outward thing, but their heart is not right, so He is asking us, the Lord.

6

"[Rather] is this not the fast which I choose,
To undo the bonds of wickedness,
To tear to pieces the ropes of the yoke,
To let the oppressed go free
And break apart every [enslaving] yoke?

It says that when you truly fast and pray, the bonds of wickedness are undone, and every yoke is torn into pieces. When we fast, pray, and seek God for the oppressed, they go free. And anything is enslaving anyone we command it broken in Jesus' name.

7

*"Is it not to divide your bread with the
hungry
And bring the homeless poor into the
house;
When you see the naked, that you cover
him,
And not to hide yourself from [the needs of]
your own flesh and blood?*

God says we need to feed the hungry and
have a good enough house for the homeless
to come, and maybe you are in church, and
you see someone who needs a particular
thing, dress, shoe or whatever it might be,
gets it for them. It is possible to hide myself
from the need of our spouses,

8

"Then your light will break out like the dawn,
And your healing (restoration, new life) will quickly spring forth;
Your righteousness will go before you [leading you to peace and prosperity],
The glory of the LORD will be your rear guard.
"Then you will call, and the LORD will answer;
You will cry for help, and He will say, 'Here I am.'
If you take away from your midst the yoke [of oppression],
The finger pointed in scorn [toward the oppressed or the godly], and [every form of] wicked (sinful, unjust) speech,

One peter 3 warns us about dwelling with our wife with understanding lest our prayers do not get answered. If you don't want hindrances to your prayers, then you must understand how God sees marriage because God is holy and righteous. He wants us to operate in certain ways and not hide from the needs of those closest to us, from our families.

We need to walk in fear of God, and I want to leave you with a question.

Do you want to walk in the power of God?

Do you want to see the glory of God in your marriage, home and family?

Or do you want to struggle for your prayers to be answered? Struggle for your needs to be met? You might say oh am fine by myself, and I am good on my own, thank you. This whole marriage thing, I don't believe in it. That's fine, and the Bible says God is not mocked. Whatsoever a man sows, that is what he will reap. We surely don't want to be on the wrong end of the stick. We want to be faithful to God. Make sure you walk in oneness with your spouse.

May the Lord bless and keep you and cause His face to shine upon you and give you peace. In the name of Jesus. God Bless you!

Printed in Great Britain
by Amazon